HELEN

Helen, the most beautiful woman in the world, the face that launched a thousand ships! Everyone has heard these superlatives regarding Helen of Troy, but few know anything more except she left her husband and ran off with a handsome prince. This booklet is designed to give a fuller picture of this most famous of women.

Helen's mortal parents were King Tyndareus of Sparta and his wife Leda. Helen, however, was also said to be the daughter of Zeus, supreme god of the ancient world. The story goes that he loved her mother Leda and turned himself into a swan for his love-making. Helen's beauty was renowned, and her skin was said to be white as a swan. It was even believed that she was hatched from an egg, and that for many centuries the shell of that egg could be seen hanging, decorated with ribbons, from the roof of a Spartan temple.

Helen's sister was Clytemnestra who married King Agamemnon of Mycenae, and Agamemnon's brother Menelaus married Helen to become king of Sparta. To win her hand Tyndareus first held a contest to which all the eligible young nobles and princes from around Greece came. They had to display their skill in wrestling, athletics and exhibit exceptional strength and endurance in various competitions. Menelaus must have shown great ability to have become the successful contender. Tyndareus, however, had made a condition of entry: they were made to swear an oath that the losers would all support the lucky winner if ever he needed their help.

So far as is known Menelaus and Helen lived happily and had a daughter Hermione. All was as it should be till one day Paris, the son of King Priam of Troy in Asia Minor, was asked to adjudicate at a contest to be held on Mt. Ida, not far from Troy. This event, famous ever after as the Judgement of Paris,* required him to choose between three goddesses as to whom he thought was the fairest. The goddesses were Hera, goddess of women and marriage; Athena, goddess of war, and of arts and crafts; and Aphrodite, goddess of love. Each tried to bribe Paris in order to be the one chosen; Hera and Athena promised him power and victory respectively, and Aphrodite offered him the most beautiful woman in the world. Paris without hesitation chose the latter.

In time Aphrodite saw to it that Paris came to the court of King Menelaus at Sparta. A banquet was held in his honour and it was there, under the influence of Aphrodite, that he first set eyes on the king's wife, the beautiful Helen. The result was an unconquerable passion. King Menelaus was conveniently called away to Crete to see to the funeral of his grandfather, and in his absence Paris broke the unwritten laws of behaviour which was never to abuse hospitality. He seduced his host's wife, and persuaded her to leave her husband and child and run away with him, taking a quantity of Spartan treasure with him. They spent their first honeymoon night on the small island of Kranae (modern Marathonisi), close by the ancient port of Sparta, today's Gythion.

What is little known about Paris is that he was already married to a nymph on Mt. Ida named Oenone. Paris had been brought up by a shepherd on the mountain because, just before his birth, his mother, Queen Hecuba, had dreamed that the baby to be born would bring about the downfall of Troy. His life is somewhat blurred between his early years on Mt. Ida as a shepherd, and later when he was reunited with his parents who seemed to have forgotten the dream.

When King Menelaus returned from Crete and found his wife gone, he appealed to his brother King Agamemnon, who rallied the Greek nobles throughout the land (the failed contenders for Helen's hand who had sworn to support Menelaus if needed). Together they amassed a great army with Agamemnon as commander-in-chief. And so they sailed for Troy with the sole purpose of retrieving Helen and recovering the treasure. It was a matter of honour.

In the tenth year of the war (and Homer's *Iliad* deals with the tenth year only) it was decided there had been enough killings, and that King Menelaus and Paris should fight it out in a duel; whoever came out the victor would take Helen together with the stolen treasure, and that would be the end of the matter. The duel was fought on the Trojan plain within sight of the citadel where King Priam and his elders looked on. Prompted by Aphrodite who put into Helen's heart a sudden longing to return to Menelaus and her homeland, she came out to watch. As she approached, King Priam pointed out her beauty to his friends: *"No one could blame the Trojans and Greek men-at-arms for suffering so long for such a woman's sake. She is fearfully like the immortal goddesses."* (Iliad 3:156-158)

The duel began and both nearly drew blood. It was when Menelaus had managed to seize Paris by the horsehair crest of his helmet and the strap under his chin was choking him to death, that Aphrodite unfairly intervened. She wrapped him in a thick mist, and carried him away, setting him down in his own 'fragrant' bedroom. Menelaus was left like a raging lion, wondering where his quarry had gone. Aphrodite then fetched Helen and brought her to Paris, and in no time they were once again in each other's arms.

The *Iliad* is full of such divine interventions, not only from Aphrodite but also from many of the Olympian gods, some fighting on the side of the Greeks, others supporting the Trojans. Because Aphrodite had been chosen by Paris as 'the fairest' at the Judgement, she naturally allied herself to his people, while both Hera and Athena supported the Greeks.

And so the Trojan War raged on, one side advancing at one moment, then the other rallying while the other retreated. At one critical moment the Trojans had driven the Greeks right back to their ships and were setting fire to them, when Achilles,* who was nursing a grudge against King Agamemnon and refusing to fight, allowed his lifelong companion Patroclus to lead his men into battle. He gave him his armour to put on in the hope that the Trojans would think he himself had returned to the war. Achilles had been greatly feared on the battlefield as he was a swift and ruthless warrior. Many Trojans were killed or, thinking Patroclus was Achilles, fled at the sight of him. But it was not to last. With the help of Apollo, Patroclus was soon to be fatally wounded by Hector, Paris' elder brother.

Achilles was so anguished by the death of his dearest friend, that he forgot his grudge and was determined only to avenge his death. Once Achilles rejoined the battle the Trojans were pushed back, fleeing before this swift-footed, enraged and fearless warrior. Hector found himself running for his life around the city walls till Achilles caught and killed him; he then tied his body behind his chariot and dragged it triumphantly around the city before the horrified eyes of Hector's family and fellow citizens.

It was Paris, this dilettante who, on the death of his brother Hector, took his own revenge and killed Achilles with an arrow in his heel, his one vulnerable spot.

Then Paris himself was killed. With his death two other sons of King Priam contested for Helen: Helenus a seer, and Deiphobus of whom little is known. Apparently, Helenus had foreseen that disaster would come when Paris sailed for Sparta, but nobody had paid attention to his warnings.

When Deiphobus married Helen, Helenus had been left jealous and angry. Because of this, when he was taken prisoner by the Greeks on Mt. Ida, he treacherously informed them how the war could be won. One of the things they should do, he told them, was to steal the *palladium* from the temple of Athena on the citadel. The *palladium* was an image of the goddess Athena which was said to have fallen from heaven and, so long as it remained in her temple, the city would always have her protection and be inviolable.

Having learned this, the great Odysseus,* often referred to by Homer as 'cunning' and 'resourceful', together with the hero Diomedes, disguised themselves as beggars and managed one night to get into the city. Helen recognized them and, instead of giving them away, helped them steal the image, and the two warriors disappeared back into the night to their camp.

It was Odysseus also who saw the advantage in the idea put to him by Helenus of a Wooden Horse.* Odysseus instructed Epeius, a master craftsman, to build this colossal structure which was to be large enough to conceal inside it thirty, some say forty, of the best Greek warriors. The plan was to leave it on the the Trojan plain in full view of the city, and for the Greeks to burn the huts beside their ships and appear to sail for home. In fact, they dropped anchor behind the nearby island of Tenedos where they lay in hiding.

It is said that on seeing the Wooden Horse Helen and her new husband Deiphobus came down to the plain and circled around it. Suspecting a ruse, Deiphobus persuaded Helen to call out the names of the Greek warriors, imitating the voices of their wives, and it had taken all Odysseus' self-discipline and persuasive powers to stop his companions from calling back to her and giving themselves away.

A Greek spy, who courageously pretended to have been left behind, allowed himself to be captured. He put on an act of the distraught prisoner who had been the intended victim of a human sacrifice but had managed to escape. He threw himself on their mercy, explaining to them how the Horse was his people's intended gift to their goddess in order to appease her for the stealing of her image, and in the hope that she would grant them a safe journey home. His acting skills were so convincing that the Trojans believed him, and King Priam ordered the Wooden Horse to be brought into the city and placed before the temple. The king and his people were overjoyed by this sudden end of hostilities. And so the Horse was trundled up into the city, and a portion of its defence walls was dismantled to allow it access.

That night the Greek fleet sailed in to Beşik bay. On a pre-arranged signal, the men hiding within the Horse were released by 'the spy', and at once the sleeping city was awakened to the sound of screams, and the crackling of timber as houses went up in flames, and the entire city was torched.

During this conflagration Menelaus came across Helen in her house. On seeing his wife, he was at first filled with rage against her. He raised his sword to kill her but Aphrodite quickly intervened. It is said that Helen was serene, and that she either lowered her garment and revealed her naked beauty to him, or she drew her veil across her face in a seductive gesture or, as some have claimed, she threw himself at his feet and clasped his knees in supplication. Whatever action she took, quite unexpectedly Menelaus was so overcome with love for her, that his sword fell from his grasp, and under her gaze all was forgiven.

With the war over, Menelaus and Helen sailed for home, but found themselves stranded in Egypt for seven years, ostensibly because Menelaus had failed to make the appropriate sacrifices to the offended gods of Troy. After seeking advice he managed to appease the gods, and he and Helen finally returned home.

Once back in Sparta Helen resumed her duties as queen and mother, and she and Menelaus lived comparatively peacefully. The spotlight fell on her again in Homer's *Odyssey* when the son of Odysseus, Telemachus, came to Sparta some years later. He wanted to find out if they knew what had happened to his father who had not yet returned from the war. Telemachus arrived when they were celebrating the wedding of their daughter, Hermione, who was to marry Neoptolemus, the son of Achilles. He was welcomed at the palace and, when Helen entered, she could see the likeness in him to Odysseus.

Homer's last mention of Helen is when Menelaus and Helen then retired to bed. In spite of all they had been through, they were now reconciled because beside Menelaus ...*lay Helen of the light robes, shining among women.* (Odyssey 4:305)

And so Helen and Menelaus lived out their natural lives together in apparent harmony. Though her husband's name is barely remembered today, Helen's image has never faded. For centuries in Sparta young girls sang and danced beside the river Eurotas at a festival in her honour. She was worshipped as a goddess, and young girls prayed to be like her, fearless and beautiful. The *Menelaon* at Sparta can today be seen which marks the site where it is believed Helen and Menelaus were finally laid to rest. The *Menelaon* itself became a shrine to this daughter of Zeus, the supreme god of the heavens, who had made love to Leda her mother, for which he had turned himself into a swan. Born of a god, it is no surprise that after her death she, the most beautiful woman in the world, was worshipped as a goddess.

* Denotes a separate booklet on the subject.

FAMILY TREE

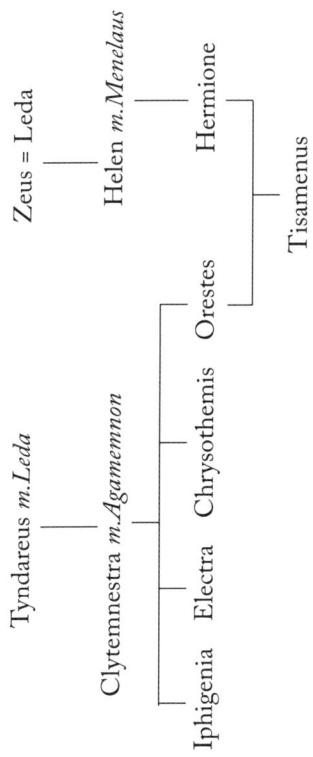

GLOSSARY OF GODS AND HEROES

ACHILLES – A major Greek hero in the Trojan War. He was the son of King Peleus of Phthia and Thetis, a sea-goddess.

AGAMEMNON – King of Mycenae and leader of the Greeks in the Trojan War.

APHRODITE – Goddess of love. She supported the Trojans in the war.

APOLLO – Son of Zeus and Leto, and twin brother of Artemis. He was god of music, archery and prophecey. He supported the Trojans in the war.

ATHENA – Daughter of Zeus. She was born from his head mature and fully armed. She was goddess of war, and arts and crafts, and was the embodiment of wisdom. She supported the Greeks in the Trojan War.

CLYTEMNESTRA – Wife of King Agamemnon.

DEIPHOBUS – Son of King Priam of Troy and his wife Hecuba. He married Helen after Paris was killed.

DIOMEDES – A great Greek warrior and companion of Odysseus.

HECTOR – Eldest son of King Priam of Troy and Hecuba.

HECUBA – Wife of King Priam, and mother of Hector, Paris, Deiphobus and Helenus.

HELEN – The beautiful wife of Menelaus, king of Sparta, who was seduced by Paris.

HELENUS – Seer son of King Priam and Hecuba.

HEPHAESTUS – Son of Zeus and Hera. He was a master blacksmith and metal-worker, creating great works of art in gold and silver. His home was Mt. Olympus.

HERA – Goddess of women and marriage. Wife of Zeus. She supported the Greeks in the war.

HERMIONE – Daughter of Helen and King Menelaus.

MENELAUS – King of Sparta, married to Helen.

ODYSSEUS – Son of Laertes, king of Ithaka. One of the finest of the Greek warriors.

OENONE – A nymph on Mt. Ida who was married to Paris.

PARIS – Son of King Priam and Hecuba. He seduced Helen.

PATROCLUS – Lifelong companion of Achilles.

PELIUS – King of Phthia, father of Achilles by Thetis.

PRIAM – King of Troy, married to Hecuba. He was the father of Paris, Hector, Deiphobus and Helenus.

TELEMACHUS – Son of Odysseus.

THETIS – A semi-divine Nereid, wife of King Peleus, and mother of Achilles.

TYNDARIUS – King of Sparta, and possible mortal father of Helen

ZEUS – Supreme god of the ancient world, and husband of Hera. He had many extra-marital affairs and was said to be the father of Helen.

MORE FROM THE
PUT IT IN YOUR POCKET SERIES

GREEK ISLAND MYTHS

ALL YOU NEED TO KNOW ABOUT
THE ISLAND'S MYTHS, LEGENDS
AND ITS GODS

CHIOS

CRETE

KOS

NAXOS

RHODES

SANTORINI

ALSO BY JILL DUDLEY

YE GODS! (TRAVELS IN GREECE)

YE GODS! II (MORE TRAVELS IN GREECE)

LAP OF THE GODS (TRAVELS IN CRETE
AND THE AEGEAN ISLANDS)